PYLON!

The Omaha Air Races
1931-1934

WALLACE C. PETERSON

Dageforde Publishing, Inc.

ISBN 1-886225-89-3
Cover illustration by Angie Johnson

Dageforde Publishing, Inc.
128 East 13th Street
Crete, Nebraska 68333

Printed in the United States of America
10 9 8 7 6 5 4 3 2 1

To the Memory of my Brother Harold

Also by Wallace C. Peterson

Income, Employment, and Economic Growth

Elements of Economics

Silent Depression: The Fate of the American Dream

Transfer Spending, Taxes, and the American Welfare State

Market Power and the Economy

Our Overloaded Economy

The Welfare State in France

Contents

Introduction

The eleven years from 1929 through 1939 were the Golden Age of American air racing—a colorful time in which a handful of bold and innovative pilots in their mostly home-built planes brought speed and excitement to the depression years. Before 1929, the National Air Races were dominated by military airplanes, but after the Travel Air Mystery Ship won the 1929 race, civilian pilots were in command. In most years the races were held at Cleveland's municipal airport over the Labor Day weekend, although in 1930 they moved to Chicago, and in 1933 and 1936, to Los Angeles. Traditionally, the Nationals were known as the Cleveland Air Races.

Two major events dominated the Nationals—the Thompson Trophy Race and the Bendix Transcontinental Trophy Race. The former was a one hundred- to two hundred-mile triangular closed course race, the crowning event of the Cleveland Races, and the latter a cross-country race from either Burbank, California, to Cleveland; or New York City to Los Angeles.

The national—and regional—air races were major proving grounds for aviation, speeding the development of aircraft design and engines, especially for the low-wing fighters of World War II. The progress in aviation design is reflected by the fact that in 1929 the average speed for the Thompson Trophy winner was 194.90 miles per hour, but by 1939 the average had risen to 282.54 miles per hour.

Along with the National Air Races, there were important regional air races during these years. Among these regionals were the Omaha Air Races, held in 1931, 1932, 1933, and 1934. With one or two exceptions, all of the major flyers and airplanes from air racing's Golden Age came to Omaha's races, normally held in the spring and summer (May 1931 and 1932, June 1933, and August 1934). The races were held at Omaha's Municipal Airport under the sponsorship of the Omaha Junior Chamber of Commerce.

As a boy (ten to thirteen years of age) I was fortunate enough to be taken by my older brother Harold to each of these races. I was at the races on Sunday, May 17, 1931, when Charles "Speed" Holman crashed to his death, and again on Sunday, August 12, 1934, when Gordon Israel's beautiful racer, *Redhead*, nosed over on landing after winning the Gene Eppley feature race. Fortunately, Israel was not hurt in this accident, although *Redhead* was severely damaged. Israel, who was twenty-three at the time of this crash, went on to have a brilliant career as an aircraft designer, working at one time or another for every major aircraft manufacturer in the United States.

The 1931-1934 Omaha Air Races were a major event in Omaha's history, but to the best of the writer's knowledge, the full story of these exciting days during the Depression in Omaha has never been told. This book seeks to remedy that.

Wallace C. Peterson
Lincoln, Nebraska, 2002

1

Air Racing Comes to Omaha

As a small boy growing up near the outskirts of North Omaha, I developed a passionate interest in airplanes. This was sparked in part by my avid addiction to the World War I stories of air fighting that were a staple of one of the pulp magazines of the era. It was also stimulated because there was a cow pasture airport on the Spanggaard Dairy, barely two blocks from our Florence Boulevard house. I spent many, many hours there watching the Travel Air biplanes, with their OX-5 engines, take off and land.

I was overjoyed when in 1931—I was then ten years old—my brother Harold told me that he was taking me to the air races, being held in Omaha for the first time. Harold was twenty-two years old, had a job working at the Union Pacific Railroad headquarters, and was an avid amateur motion picture photographer. Harold graduated from Omaha Central High School in 1927, but unlike my older brother Murray, he did not go on to college after completing high school. He had a good job in the engineering department of the Union Pacific, owned a small red Chevrolet coupe, was living at home, and secretly taking flying lessons at Omaha's Muny airport. Since we were not a church-going family, Harold found it relatively easy to take his flying lessons on Sunday mornings without my parents discovering what he was doing. This is how I got my first airplane ride. One Sunday in May, Harold took me to the airport, and along with his instructor, we went flying. I was hooked, determined more than ever to become a pilot.

We flew in a high-wing monoplane, a Curtis-Robin. It was the same type of airplane that Wrong Way Corrigan made famous when he flew from New York to England, after telling authorities, who forbade him to make the transatlantic flight, that he was returning home to California. When confronted by the irate aviation authorities after landing in England, he said he must "…have made a wrong turn." Forever after, he was known as Wrong Way Corrigan. In the Curtis-Robin, the pilot sat in front, behind the instrument panel, and the two passengers the airplane could carry sat directly behind the pilot.

In May 1931, when Omaha held its first air races, the nation was sliding into the worst economic depression in its history. At that time, the Depression—destined to last ten years—was sixteen and one-half months old; by the end of the year, the national output had fallen by 15.9 percent and prices by 38.1 percent, while unemployment had climbed to 15.9 percent of the labor force. The fall in output, prices, and employment would not reach bottom until 1933, when a turnaround began after unemployment nationally reached a record breaking 24.9 percent of the labor force.

Omaha, of course not immune from this national malaise, was suffering along with the rest of the nation. In 1932 Nebraska—traditionally a Republican state—cast 64.1 percent of its vote for Franklin D. Roosevelt in the presidential election, and 53.3 percent for Democrat Charles W. Bryan over Republican Dwight Griswold in the race for governor. Democratic domination of state politics would continue until the end of the 1930s.

About the only good thing that can be said about the early years of the Depression was that food was exceedingly cheap. An advertisement by the A&P Grocery on May 16, 1931—the

2

second day of the air races—listed a pork loin roast at twelve cents a pound, two pounds of butter for forty-three cents, eggs at fifteen cents a dozen, coffee at nineteen cents a pound, two large packages of Post Toasties™ for twenty-three cents, a one-pint box of fresh strawberries for ten cents, ten bars of soap for twenty-seven cents, and a ten-pound bag of sugar at forty-nine cents.

Omaha's population in 1931 was 214,000; that of Douglas County, 232,000; and Nebraska, 1,372,963. The mayor of Omaha was R.L. Metcalfe, and the state's two U.S. senators were George W. Norris and Robert A. Howell. Both were Republicans, although Senator Norris later became an Independent. At that time, the city had two daily newspapers, the *Omaha World-Herald* and the *Omaha Bee-News*. Both papers published morning and evening editions.

Air Racing in America

To put Omaha's air races of the early 1930s in perspective, it is necessary to say something about the overall status of air racing in America, especially in the Depression years of the 1930s. Air meets, where pilots and their planes gathered to compete in races and aerobatics and entertain awe stricken spectators, are almost as old as the airplane itself. But the real beginnings of modern air racing, especially the National Air Races held in Cleveland, Ohio, for many years, trace back to two meets in the fall of 1921—one in Kansas City, Missouri, and the other in Omaha, Nebraska. These meets were held in conjunction with the International Aero Congress, and featured the second Pulitzer Trophy Race. The latter, one of the mainstays of the early days of air racing, was established in 1920 by Ralph Herbert and Joseph Pulitzer Jr. The Kansas City meet was held first, and after that meet the pilots flew their planes to Omaha to compete. For these early races, the planes had to have a speed of at least 140 miles per hour, while the pilots had

3

to have their F.A.I. (Fédération Aéronautique Internationale) licenses and had to be registered with the Aero Club of America.

The National Air Races actually got their start the following year (1922) when they were held at Detroit, where they had six major events. Included in the Detroit meet was a twenty-mile closed course aerial water derby, in which the planes were required to land and taxi on the water in the fifth, sixth, and seventh laps. This race was won by a U.S. Navy plane. Actually, throughout the 1920s the National Air Races were dominated by military planes. It was not until 1929, when the *Travel Air Mystery Ship* won the Thompson Trophy Race, that the military's lock on top prizes in the races was broken.

In 1923 the National Air Races were held in St. Louis, and in the following year at Wilber Wright Field in Dayton, Ohio. The next year (1925), they moved to Mitchell Field, Long Island, New York, when two French army planes entered the race for the Liberty Engine Builders Trophy that had been established in 1922. The French entry gave the races an international aspect for the first time. In 1926 the races were held at Philadelphia in conjunction with the 150th anniversary of the signing of the Declaration of Independence. For the first time, the races were entirely under civilian supervision, and of the nineteen events, fourteen were for civilian flyers only. This year, the Pulitzer Race was not on the program. Some observers said this was the reason for poor attendance since the weather was not particularly good. Felts Field in Spokane, Washington, was the site of the 1927 races. The next year they were held in Los Angeles, and with respect to attendance and revenue collected, were the most successful aerial contests ever held in the United States up to that time.

Omaha's Municipal Airport

Omaha's Municipal Airport in 1931 was not the modern air terminal that it is today. The field was basically grass with dirt runways. For the air races, oil was poured onto the runways and then rolled to make the surface reasonably hard. At the airport there were three hangars for three separate companies. To the south was the hangar for Rapid Air Service, a company that for a brief period operated an airline (Rapid Airlines) between Omaha, St. Joseph, and Kansas City, Missouri. Unfortunately, the airline went out of business when its main airliner, a Stinson Trimotor, crashed on a flight between St. Joseph and Omaha during a thunderstorm. All on board were killed. In spite of the accident, the company survived, becoming what is called in aviation circles a fixed base operation and providing airplane rides, flight instruction, and charter services. Immediately to the north of the Rapid Air Service facility was the hangar for Mid-West Aviation, another fixed base operator. Then, at the north end of the field was the Boeing Air Transport repair depot and passenger terminal. Boeing Air Transport was the grandfather of the contemporary United Airlines. The main route for Boeing Air Transport was from San Francisco to Chicago, with major stops in Salt Lake City, Cheyenne, and Omaha. On this route, Boeing Air Transport flew trimotor, fabric-covered Boeing 80-A biplanes with two pilots and twelve passengers. It was on the Boeing 80-A that Boeing Air Transport introduced stewardesses—or hostesses, as they were originally called—to the flying public. For the Omaha Air Races, a grandstand that could seat fifteen thousand was erected between the Rapid Air and Mid-West hangars, only fifty to seventy-five yards west of the north-south runway. Until 1959, Omaha's airport was known as the Omaha Municipal Airport, but then the name was changed to Eugene Eppley Airfield.

City Commissioner Dean Noyes was the commissioner in charge of the airport, and also served as chairman of the Omaha Air Race Board. A strong-minded individual, Commissioner

Noyes got into a major tiff with the Junior Chamber of Commerce over the special seating section he had set up for four hundred of his cronies in front of the Boeing hangar and only a few hundred feet away from the north-south runway. Rather than risk an outright break with the commissioner over his action, members of the Junior Chamber held their tongues, but complained privately. The *Omaha World-Herald* asked editorially, "Since when, we may ask, has our impulsive commissioner secured for himself a commission as the Mussolini of the airport?" In spite of the creation and criticism of the Dean Noyes Section, the newspaper, the Junior Chamber, and other critics complimented the Commissioner on the excellent job he had done in planning and organizing Omaha's first air race. As a city commissioner, Noyes received $4,500 a year, which in 2002 prices would equal $35,139. The current salary for an Omaha city councilman (which a commissioner is now called) is $26,423 per year.

Army Fliers Arrive

Omahans received a special pre-air racing treat on Tuesday, May 12, when sixty-seven fighter planes from the Army Air Corps made an overnight stop on a flight from California to National Air Corps maneuvers in Dayton, Ohio. The planes, which were Boeing P-12Cs from the 20th Pursuit Group, flew in formations of three over downtown Omaha at three thousand feet, before circling and landing at the municipal airport. The P-12C was an open cockpit biplane with 425-horsepower, twelve-cylinder Wasp engine that could attain a maximum speed of 190 miles per hour. They were accompanied by nine transport airplanes, which carried sixty-three enlisted men to service the fighters. Major Clarence L. Tinker, for whom Tinker Field in Oklahoma is named, was in command of the group. When the three squadrons that formed the group departed Omaha on Wednesday, they gathered into V-shaped formations and headed for their next stop, Rantoul, Illinois. On Tues-

Traffic Mapped to and From Air Races

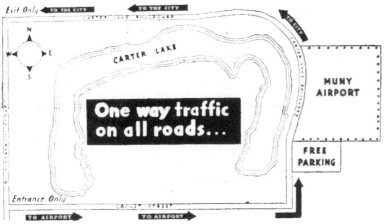

day night, the officers flying the planes were guests at a dinner hosted by the Omaha Chamber of Commerce. The sixty-seven fighter planes that landed at Omaha represented one-tenth of the Army Air Corps' fighter strength. Omaha newspapers reported that five thousand spectators turned out to greet the army fliers as they landed at Omaha.

In other pre-racing news, it was announced by M.M. Meyers, president of the Omaha Air Race Association, that a Pitcairn auto-giro, an ungainly ancestor of the modern helicopter, would make its first appearance west of the Mississippi River. The plane, which was similar to the one that landed on the White House lawn to receive the Collier Trophy from President Hoover, was to come from Poughkeepsie, New York, and to be flown by John Miller. The Collier Trophy was awarded for the most significant contribution to flying during 1930. Meyers also said that Dorothy Hester, a nineteen-year-old woman pilot from Portland, Oregon, would come to the Omaha races and attempt to break the world's record for consecutive barrel rolls. At that time, she was the only woman pilot to execute an outside loop successfully.

Omaha's first air races opened at 1:30 in the afternoon on Friday as Governor Charles W. Bryan led off the airport dedication ceremonies. Others present in the guest box were John Hopkins, mayor of Omaha; C. N. Wilhelm, King of Ak-Sar-Ben; Miss Marcelle Folda, Queen of Ak-Sar-Ben; Rev. E.J. Flanagan of Boys Town; and M.M. Meyers, Omaha's "first citizen."

2

Racing Planes and Racing Pilots

The air races of the 1930s, including the Nationals at Cleveland, were not just about racing. They were air shows, designed not only to showcase the spectacular racing planes of the era, but also to include aerobatics, parachute jumping, army maneuvers, balloon busting and bomb dropping contests, glider flights, and demonstrations of new aircraft.

The five-mile race course at Omaha was a triangle (see map), with a seventy-five-foot black and orange pylon at each corner of the triangle. Most of the races were for twenty-five miles, which meant flying five times around the triangular course. The main pylon and finishing line were just off the north-south runway, directly in front of the main grandstand. After rounding this pylon, the race planes headed to the northeast for pylon number two, which was just across the Missouri River in Iowa. From here they flew due west to pylon number three, where they turned south to roar past the grandstand for another lap or to the finish line. The racing planes flew at an altitude of fifty to one hundred feet, barely skimming over the trees that lay to the north and east of the airport. The pylon turns were the most spectacular part of any race, as the racing planes went around the pylons in near-vertical banks, bunched

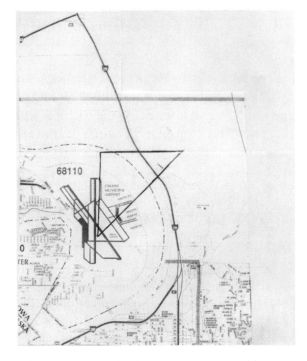

City of Omaha.

closely together, especially near the start of the race. Each race began with a horse race start, as planes were lined up horizontally across the field, waiting for the starting signal.

The Racing Pilots

Except for the legendary Roscoe Turner, later the three-time winner of the Thompson Trophy Race at Cleveland, the Omaha Air Races in the early 1930s attracted nearly all of the well-known racing pilots of that era. Most of the pilots flew into Omaha in their racing planes on Thursday, May 14, 1931, the day before the start of the races. Racing pilots arriving on Thursday included Al Williams, Stub Quimby, Johnny Livingston, Bill Ong, Art Davis, Art Chester, Harold Neumann, Roger Don Rae, and Roy Brown.

A late arrival was Charles "Speed" Holman, who flew in from Minneapolis on Saturday, May 16, just in time to enter the twenty-five mile free-for-all race, which he won with an average speed of 153.84 miles per hour. Jimmy Doolittle, also a winner of the Thompson Trophy Race and leader of the famed air raid on Tokyo in 1942, flew into Omaha from St. Louis with his wife and James H. Haizlip, another racing pilot. Doolittle did not enter the Omaha races. Benny Howard, one of the legendary greats of the Golden Age of air racing, did not fly in, but brought his tiny racer *Pete* to the race meet by truck from St. Louis. *Pete* was flown in the Omaha races by Bill Ong. Later Ong gave the crowd an unexpected thrill when the engine of *Pete* blew up. Fortunately, he was able to trade speed for altitude, bringing the tiny racer to a safe dead-stick landing.

The air racing pilots of the thirties were a close knit, though highly competitive, group. Most of them designed and built their own planes. Sometimes they had sponsors, but usually they had to scrounge for the money to finance their planes. Prize money was obviously an important income source. Some of them, like Harold Neumann, started out as a barnstormer in the 1920s, and some of them, also like Neumann, eventually became airline pilots. Harold Neumann's career as a racing pilot began in 1928, just a year after he learned to fly. During his air racing career, he flew in the Greve, Shell, and Thompson races, being named the nation's number one racing pilot in 1935. In 1936 he began a thirty-year career with Trans World Airlines (TWA), during which he flew as a captain on DC-2, DC-3, Boeing Stratoliner, Boeing 707, and Lockheed Constellation aircraft.

Benny Howard, also an airline pilot and one of the best of the Golden Age race pilots, designed and built four of the most celebrated racing planes of the 1930s: *Pete, Ike, Mike,* and *Mr. Mulligan.* All of Howard's planes carried the designation "DGA" which Howard said stood for "Damned Good Airplane." In 1935 Benny Howard flew *Mr. Mulligan* to victory in the Bendix Trophy Race from Los Angeles to Cleveland, while

11

two days later Harold Neumann won the Thompson Trophy Race in the same airplane. *Mr. Mulligan* was the only airplane to win both the Bendix and Thompson races. Unfortunately, *Mr. Mulligan* was destroyed the following year when it crashed in a New Mexican desert while Benny Howard, with his wife Maxine as co-pilot, were flying in the 1936 Bendix Race from New York to Los Angeles. The cause of the crash was the loss of a blade from the plane's three-bladed propeller. Both Benny Howard and his wife were badly injured in the crash. Fortunately, they both recovered, and Benny Howard went on to have a distinguished career with several major aircraft manufacturers.

Another outstanding and colorful pilot from the Golden Age was Art Chester from Joliet, Illinois. Born in 1899, Chester learned to fly in 1921, when he was twenty-two years old. After a stint of barnstorming in the 1920s, he became the manager of Wilhelmi Airport near Joliet, where in his spare time he designed, built, and flew racing airplanes. He was instrumental in the organization of the Professional Race Pilots' Association, a group dedicated to the design and construction of small racing planes. Chester died in a crash in 1949, when he apparently lost control of his racing plane, *Swee' Pea*, while rounding a pylon during the American Gold Cup Races in San Diego, California. He was forty-nine years old.

Undoubtedly, the dean of the air racing pilots from the 1930s was Steve Wittman of Oshkosh, Wisconsin, a tall, lanky, bespectacled man who looked more like a scholarly professor than an air racing pilot. Born in 1904, Steve Wittman was still racing when he was in his eighties; unfortunately he was killed on April 27, 1995, when he and his wife were returning from the Miami Air Races. Although the exact cause of the crash that killed Wittman and his wife has never been determined, it appears that fabric on the wing of the home-built plane he was flying came loose. During his long career in air racing, Wittman designed and built a number of well-known racing airplanes, the most famous of which were *Chief Oshkosh* and *Bonzo*. Both were mid-wing monoplanes, which Wittman flew in the Nationals and most of the regional air races during the 1930s. After World War II, Wittman designed a high-wing, two-place monoplane, called a Tailwind, a favorite home-built airplane for many years of members of the Experimental Aircraft Association. It was a Tailwind that Wittman and his wife were flying when they were killed. When Wittman was not flying in air races, he was manager of the Winnebago County Airport at Oshkosh, which in 1969 was renamed Wittman Field in his honor. Steve Wittman's achievements are especially remarkable, for he was practically blind in one eye—today he probably would not be able get an airplane pilot's license. Wittman described his airplane design philosophy as "KISS—Keep It Simple, Stupid."

The Racing Planes

As colorful as the pilots who designed and built the racing planes of the 1930s—were the airplanes themselves. Almost without exception, the racing planes were essentially home built. The closest to factory built planes were the Gee Bee racers, built by the Granville Brothers of Springfield, Massachusetts, and the Laird Solutions, designed and built by Emil M. "Matty" Laird, who formed the M.E. Laird Airplane Company in Chicago in 1919. In 1930 Charles "Speed" Holman flew a Laird Solution to victory in the Thompson Trophy Race. It was the first and only biplane to win that race. In 1931 a Gee Bee flown by Lowell Bayles won the Thompson Trophy Race.

The stubby, barrel shaped Gee Bee racers are probably the best known of the racing airplanes of the 1930s. Zantford D. "Granny" Granville and his four brothers set up a factory in an old dance hall in Springfield, Massachusetts, where they first designed and built a little sports biplane. When sales dried up in the Depression, their chief engineer, Bob Hall, suggested they build a racing plane to bring home some cash for their firm. Their first racing plane, designated Model Z and named the *City of Springfield,* was fifteen feet long, with a twenty-three-foot wingspread, and was powered by a 535-horsepower Pratt and Whitney Wasp Junior engine. Painted yellow with black trim, the Model Z had a top speed of 270 miles per hour. In 1931 Lowell Bayles won the Thompson Trophy Race in this airplane at an average speed of 240 miles per hour. Unfortunately, Lowell Bayles was killed in December of that year when the Gee Bee Model Z crashed near Detroit during Bayles' attempt to set a land speed record. The crash happened because a gas cap came loose and smashed through the windshield, causing Bayles to lose control of the airplane. The plane, which was flying at 150 feet above the ground, nosed up sharply, and the outer half of the right wing folded back. After doing two and one-half snap rolls, the Gee Bee Z crashed, bursting into a ball of flame. Bayles was killed instantly.

Following the demise of the Model Z, the Granville brothers built two more Gee Bees, labeled Super Sportsters, painted white with red trim, and decorated with dice numbers seven and eleven. Nicknamed the *Bumblebees*, the R-1 and R-2 Gee Bees were fatter and stubbier than the Model Z, and were powered by eight hundred-horsepower Pratt and Whitney Wasp Senior engines. Their top speed was 309 miles per hour. In 1932 Jimmy Doolittle won the Thompson Trophy Race in Number *11* and also set a new land speed record while at Cleveland. Unhappily, in the following year, both Gee Bees were destroyed. During the 1933 Bendix Race, Russell Boardman was killed when Gee Bee Number *11* crashed on takeoff at Indianapolis, and later in the year Gee Bee Number *7* was destroyed when it ground looped while landing at a field in Connecticut. In this crash, the pilot, Jimmy Haizlip, was not injured. This crash ended the racing careers of the two original Gee Bee Super Sportsters. In spite of the killer reputation of the R-1 and R-2 Gee Bees, Delmar Benjamin, a contemporary member of the Experimental Aircraft Association, has built and flown successfully for a number of years a full scale replica of these historic planes.

The Travel Air
"Mystery Ship" Racers

Travel Air "Mystery Ship"

Gordon Israel's **Redhead**

Miles and Atwood, Miss Los Angeles

Wallace C. Peterson

Charles Holman and his Laird Solution

Clayton Folkert's SK-3

Art Chester's Jeep

Steve Wittman's Bonzo

Steve Wittman's Bonzo

Clayton Folkert's Special Toots

Benny Howard's Mr. Mulligan

Lawrence Brown's Miss Los Angeles

Wallace C. Peterson

Benny Howard's Ike and Mike

Miles and Atwood Special

Schoenfeldt Firecracker

Benny Howard's Pete

Gee Bee Super Sportster

Almost as famous as the Gee Bee racers, were the planes designed and built by Benny Howard: *Pete, Ike, Mike,* and *Mr. Mulligan.* The first of the Howard racers, *Pete,* was designed and built in 1930 at a cost of just twenty-five hundred dollars ($15,995 in 2002 prices). It was a low-wing, open cockpit racer powered by a ninety-horsepower Wright Gypsy engine. The plane was so diminutive that Howard could barely squeeze into the tiny cockpit. In spite of its tiny size and low power, Benny Howard flew it to a third place finish in the 1930 Thompson Trophy Race at the National Air Races, held in Chicago that year. He flew at an average speed of 162.8 miles per hour. In 1931 he again flew *Pete* in the Thompson Trophy Race at Cleveland, this time coming in sixth, with an average speed of 163.5 miles per hour. This was the year that Lowell Bayles won the Thompson Race in the Gee Bee Model Z.

After *Pete,* Benny Howard designed and built two almost identical racers, *Ike* and *Mike.* Menasco engines powered both, but *Mike* had the greater horsepower—225 versus 160 for *Ike.* Both airplanes were low-wing, with a wingspan of just twenty feet and a length of seventeen feet. They were open cockpit planes, fabric covered with a fixed landing gear and wheel pants. Like *Pete,* both planes were white with black lettering. *Ike* carried the racing number thirty-nine, while *Mike* was numbered

Gordon Israel

thirty-eight. In the 1932 Thompson race, *Ike,* flown by Bill Ong, placed seventh at an average speed of 191.1 miles per hour. In the next year, 1933, Roy Minor flew *Mike* to a third place finish. In this race, *Mike* averaged 199.9 miles per hour, the highest speed yet attained by either of the racers.

In 1934 Benny Howard was joined by Gordon Israel in the design and construction of his fourth racing plane, the high-wing, enclosed cabin, Mr. Mulligan. Howard had first met Israel in 1930, when Israel was an eighteen-year-old engineering student at the Van

Hoffman Aircraft School at Lambert Field in St. Louis. The plane's five hundred- horsepower Pratt and Whitney Wasp Senior engine gave Mr. *Mulligan* a top speed of 287 miles per hour. In 1935 Benny Howard flew Mr. *Mulligan* to first place in the Bendix transcontinental race, and at the Cleveland races, Harold Neumann won first place in Mr. *Mulligan* in the Thompson Trophy Race, making Mr. *Mulligan,* as noted earlier, the only airplane to win both these races in the same year! Howard received $4,500 ($35,139 in 2002 prices) for winning the Bendix Race and $6,750 ($52,709 in 2002 prices) for winning the Thompson Race. Unfortunately, as was noted earlier, Mr. *Mulligan* crashed during the 1936 Bendix Race.

Another set of colorful planes which came to the Omaha races were the Wedell-Williams Specials—racers that won the Bendix Race in 1932 and 1933, and the Thompson Race in 1933 and 1934. These racers were designed and built by Jimmy Wedell, who had only a ninth grade education, was not able to read a blueprint, and was denied pilot training by both the Army and the Navy. Nevertheless, he became one of the most prolific designers and builders of racing planes in the 1930s. The Williams of the Wedell-Williams partnership was a wealthy New Orleans businessman who backed Wedell in the establishment of the Wedell-Williams Flying Service in 1928, and in the building of his racing planes. Wedell built his famous racers by eye, first sketching the design out on the floor of his hangar, and then beginning the actual construction.

The two most famous Wedell-Williams airplanes were Number 44, which Wedell flew to first place in the 1933 Thompson Race, and Number 57, flown to victory in the 1934 Thompson by the legendary Roscoe Turner. Number 44, painted black with red trim, had a 985-horsepower Pratt and Whitney Wasp Junior motor. Number 44 was named after the legendary .44 caliber six-gun of the Old West, because Wedell said, the airplane was "hot as a .44 and twice as fast." This airplane, which won more races than any other airplane of this era, established a world land speed record of 305.3 miles per hour in September 1933. Number 57, black with white trim, had a one thousand-horsepower Hornet engine. Its average speed in the 1934 Thompson Race was 248.1 miles per hour. Wedell-Williams racers won first, second, and third places in the 1932 Bendix Race; and first and second in both the 1933 and 1934 Bendix Races. Wedell-Williams Number 57, flown by Roscoe Turner, placed second in the 1935 Bendix. Unhappily, Jimmy Wedell didn't live to see and enjoy Turner's 1935 Bendix victory, as he was killed in 1934 when a student froze at the controls of a plane in which Wedell was teaching him to fly. A year later Harry Williams was killed in the crash of a Beechcraft plane which lost power on a takeoff at Baton Rouge.

One of the most popular and aesthetically pleasing racers of the 1930s was Art Chester's *Jeep,* named after a character in the Popeye comic strip. The graceful *Jeep* was a mid-wing monoplane with wheel pants attached to cantilever landing gear struts that flared out from the fuselage. Built in 1932 with a 225-horsepower Menasco engine, the plane had a wingspan of

only sixteen feet, eight inches, which made it one of the smallest of the racing planes of the 1930s. Originally, the *Jeep* carried the number fifteen and was painted green with white trim, but after Chester installed a new wing in 1935, the plane was painted a pale cream with dark green trim and carried the racing number three. Chester entered his plane in all of the Thompson races between 1933 and 1936, but the best the little racer did was a sixth-place finish in 1936. Art Chester and the *Jeep* rarely finished first in any of the air races Chester entered between 1933 and

Art Chester

1937, but in these five years the *Jeep* earned from lesser finishes thirty thousand dollars in prize money—a decent return on the original five thousand dollars cost to build the plane. By 1937

Roger Don Rae

modifications had brought the *Jeep* to its peak performance, so with no practical way to make it go faster, Chester decided to build a new racer. The result was again a mid-wing racer with a retractable landing gear, named *The Goon*, after another Popeye character. At the 1938 Cleveland races, Chester in *The Goon* won the Greve Race, but was forced out on the twentieth lap of the Thompson Race when his engine began to throw oil. In 1939, the last of the Nationals because of outbreak of World War II, Chester again won the Greve Race in *The Goon*, but as in Cleveland the year before, he was again forced out of the Thompson Race with an oil leak.

Joe Jacobson

Another group of racing planes was designed and constructed by Keith Rider. Between 1930 and 1938, six Keith Rider Specials were built, being designated R-1 through R-6. These planes were powered by either inline or radial engines, were covered by either plywood or fabric, had both fixed and retractable landing gear, and were owned and flown by several different racing pilots, including Roger Don Rae, Rudy Kling, Tony LeVier, and Earl Ortman. They also sported a variety of names such as *San Francisco, Bumblebee, Firecracker, Jackrabbit,* and *Eightball.* On the national scene, a Keith Rider R-1 flown by Roger Don Rae came in fifth in the 1934 Thompson Race and took third place in the 1935 Thompson, again flown by Roger Don Rae. In 1936 Keith Rider's R-3 and R-4 placed second and third in the Thompson Race. Earl Ortman flew R-3 and Roger Don Rae R-4. Keith Rider's last victory came in 1938 when Joe Jacobson flew the R-6 *Eightball* to a sixth-place finish in the Thompson Trophy Race.

Lee Miles

Three other popular racing planes from the 1930s were the Miles and Atwood Special, Clayton Folkerts SK-3, and Gordon Israel's *Redhead*. After a stint of barnstorming and stunt flying for the movies, Lee Miles opened a small airport in San Bernadino, California. In the spring of 1933, he got together with his friend Leon Atwood, an associate of Larry Brown, and the three of them designed and built the diminutive racer with a sixteen-foot eight-inch wingspan in time to enter the 1933 National Air Races, held in Los Angeles July 1-4. Painted a bright green with a silver-outlined black number six racing number, it was entered in eight races, winning first place in two, second place in two, fourth place in one, and fifth place in two. All told, Lee Miles earned fourteen hundred dollars ($8,956 in 2002 prices) at the 1933 Nationals. In the 1934 Nationals at Cleveland, Miles flying the Miles and Atwood Special came away with six first place wins, including the prestigious Greve Trophy Race top honor. In 1934 Miles was named the number one racing pilot in the nation by the National Aeronautic Association. Unfortunately, Lee Miles was instantly killed during a qualifying run at the Cleveland Nationals when a flying wire snapped while he was making a tight pylon turn.

Clayton Folkerts first gained fame as the designer and builder of the Monocoupe, a plane that such illustrious pilots as Johnny Livingston, Harold Neumann, Stub Quimby, Vern Roberts and others flew in racing and stunting competitions. In the early 1930s he began to build a series of racing planes, each one carrying the designation SK-1, SK-2, and so on. The most famous of his planes was the SK-3, named *Jupiter*. Flown by Rudy Kling, it won both the Greve and Thompson trophy races at the 1937 Cleveland Nationals. Kling was the only American racing pilot to win both the Thompson and Greve races in the same year with the same airplane. The SK planes were mid-wing

31

monoplanes with retractable landing gear, usually powered by six-cylinder Menasco engines. In December 1937 Rudy Kling took *Jupiter* to the winter All-American Races in Miami, where Kling was killed when *Jupiter* crashed after a high-speed stall at the first pylon turn. Another race pilot, Frank Haines, was also killed in the same race. After the crash of SK-3, Folkerts built another plane for the 1938 Nationals. SK-4 was almost a twin of SK-3, but at the 1938 races it developed severe wing flutter and did not compete in any of the races. In 1939, SK-4, cured of its wing flutter, returned to Cleveland, but crashed during a test flight when it stalled out as the pilot, Del Bush, tried to turn back to the field when the engine began to run rough. Bush was killed.

After the loss of SK-4, Folkerts did not build any more racing planes. In 1940 he went to work for Waco Aircraft in Troy, Ohio, helping to design gliders and trainers for the war effort. He worked there until 1948 when he and his wife moved to a farm near Iowa Falls, Iowa, where he lived until his death in 1965 at the age of sixty-seven.

In 1933, Gorden Israel, who worked with Benny Howard in the design and construction of *Mr. Mulligan*, designed, built, and flew his own racer. Named *Redhead*, his plane was a low-wing monoplane, powered by an inverted Menasco engine, with a wingspan of twenty-one feet, six inches, and an overall length of eighteen feet, six inches. Painted white with a brilliant red nose and trim, *Redhead*, with its gull-wing, was one of the most graceful of the racing planes of the 1930s. In the 1933 Nationals at Los Angeles, Gordon Israel in *Redhead* took third place in five events. However, disaster overtook Israel and *Redhead* in August 1934 at the Omaha Air Races. On Sunday, the last day of the races, Israel flying *Redhead* won the fifty-mile free-for-all Gene Eppley Trophy Race. Second place in this race went to Lee Miles, while Art Chester took third, and Roger Don Rae fourth. On landing, *Redhead* bounced about ten feet in the air, then the right landing gear buckled when the plane came down, causing the plane to nose over, coming to rest on its back.

Israel was unhurt, being speedily cut from the plane by the rescue crew. At the time of the crash, twenty-three-year-old Israel was the world's youngest professional racing pilot. In the race, for which Israel received nine hundred dollars ($7,187 in 2002 prices) for his first place win, he averaged 197.3 miles per hour. In accepting the trophy at the speaker's stand, Israel said, "Folks, I don't want you to get the wrong idea of aviation from this. When you fly these racing planes you've got to expect things like this now and then. Thanks for the trophy. It's the first trophy I ever won, and I'm pretty tickled to get it." On Monday after the races, Israel took a United Airlines plane to Cleveland to help Benny Howard get a plane ready for the National Air Races. *Redhead* was never rebuilt. When the war came, Israel went to work for Grumman Aircraft, and then later worked for Lockheed and Lear Aviation.

Three Days of Racing

Omaha's first annual air races opened on Friday, May 15, 1931, under clear skies, with a mild temperature, and a light, westerly wind. Fifty-seven different events were scheduled for the three-day show, which featured not only air racing, but also aerobatics, balloon busting contests, glider flights, dead-stick landing competition, bomb dropping events, parachute jumping contests, night flying demonstrations, and appearances by Army and Navy airplanes. Events got under way at ten o'clock each morning and lasted until half past nine at night when a fireworks display closed the program.

On the first two days there were eight races—three on the opening Friday and five on Saturday, including a free-for-all, open only to women. Air races are classified by the cubic inches of piston displacement by the airplane engines, ranging from two hundred cubic inches of displacement (the smallest engines) to one thousand cubic inches of displacement. The free-for-all races were open to engines of any displacement.

Gordon Israel's **Redhead** *noses over on landing.*

On the opening day, Johnny Livingston of Aurora, Illinois, flying a Monocoupe, won three of the four speed events. Bill Ong, flying Benny Howard's *Pete*, gave the crowd its greatest thrill when the engine on his tiny racer blew up. Trading speed for altitude, Ong was able to climb high enough to bring his plane to a safe dead-stick landing at the airport. A second close call took place on Saturday in the race for planes powered by OX-5 engines, a classic engine used by many planes in the 1920s and early 1930s. A Curtis-Robin flown by E.I. Niebeck of Grinnell, Iowa, lost a left wheel when his landing gear scraped the ground while rounding the pylon in front of the grandstand. Fortunately, Niebeck was able to make a one-wheel landing with minimum damage to his plane. Other pilots winning races in 1931 included Art Davis, Art Chester, Charles "Speed" Holman, and Harold Neumann. Holman flew in from Minneapolis on Saturday, just in time to enter the free-for-all. Because he didn't know the course, he took off last and followed the other planes around the course for the first lap. Then, he pulled into the lead and won the race with an average speed of 153.84 miles per hour. Holmes flew his Laird Solution, R-7087, the plane in which he crashed to his death on the following Sunday. In this race, Art Davis took second place; George Livingston, third; and Stub Quimby, fourth.

Another exciting event was the attempt by nineteen-year-old Dorothy Hestor of Portland, Oregon, to set two records for women flyers. She succeeded both times. On Friday, she set a record of fifty-six inverted barrel rolls, and on Sunday she set an outside loop record for women with sixty-two loops. The record for men at that time was seventy-eight loops, held by Tex Rankin. An outside loop is an extremely stressful maneuver for both the pilot and the plane. Starting from level flight, the pilot pushes the control stick forward to put the plane in a dive, and holds the stick in this position while the plane noses over, enters the bottom of the loop upside down, and then climbs back to the horizontal level. Unlike a normal, inside loop, centrifugal forces tend to push the pilot outside the airplane.

Still another crowd pleaser at the 1931 races was the appearance of a Pitcairn auto-giro, the ancestor of the modern day helicopter, and one of the strangest looking aircraft ever built. This was the first time this aircraft had been seen west of the Mississippi River. Flown by Johnny Miller, it arrived from Poughkeepsie, New York, at 3:40 Saturday afternoon. The giro had an ordinary fuselage, tail section, but a very narrow, low-wing with no lifting power. The latter came from four narrow rotors with an airfoil shape mounted by a three-legged pedestal above the fuselage. Through a gear arrangement, the rotors were connected with the giro's engine so that when the plane was ready to take off, power could be applied to turn the rotors, which then generated the lift for the giro to take off. Once the plane was in flight, the power was disconnected, but the rotors continued to turn and provide lift on their own as the plane moved through the air. The rotors—or blades—were adjustable with respect to the angle at which they met the air as they turned. By adjusting this angle, the auto-giro could climb or descend. In a demonstration flight soon after arriving, the giro flew over downtown Omaha, descended, and hovered within a few feet of the roofs of several buildings, hovered briefly over the grandstand at the airport, and then made a leisurely landing. After the demonstration flight, the giro took passengers for rides, two at a time. One of the first passengers was W. Dale Clark, president of the Omaha National Bank, who said after the flight that "...it felt safer than any other plane." Johnny Miller piloted the plane, which battled headwinds on its flight from Des Moines, and held its ground speed to sixty-five miles per hour.

Tex Rankin of Portland, Oregon, put on a spectacular aerobatics performance, climbing to more than five thousand feet, and then descending in a series of outside loops, rolls, and an inverted spin, and winding up his routine with a "falling leaf," a maneuver in which the airplane seems totally out of control. In the parachute jumping contest, several jumpers landed almost at the center of the target, but a sudden burst of wind carried one jumper into the trees at the north end of the airport. The jumps started at one thousand feet. The balloon busting contest involved pilots setting a balloon loose from their planes, and then trying to burst them with their propellers. Johnny Livingston in his Monocoupe won first place in this contest, bursting his balloon in nine seconds. Roger Rae of East Lansing, Michigan, followed him, flying a Bull Pup, and bursting his balloon in eleven and one-half seconds.

The three-day show ended on a sad note, when Charles "Speed" Holman crashed to his death a few hundred feet in front of the spectators seated in front of the Boeing hangar. The details of Holman's ill-fated flight are in the next chapter.

Financially, Omaha's first annual Air Race just about broke even, the Omaha Air Race Meet Association reported at the end of May. Receipts totaled $29,327 ($187,622 in 2002 prices) and expenses $29,290 ($187,355 in 2002 prices) for a net profit of thirty-seven dollars ($238 in 2002 prices). The Air Race manager, Phil Henderson, was paid two thousand dollars ($12,795 in 2002 prices) for three months' work. Attendance averaged between fifteen thousand and twenty thousand persons each day. M.M. Meyers, president of the Air Race Association, announced the air races would be held again in 1932, and he hoped that they could be made an annual event.

3

Death in the Afternoon

Omaha's first annual air races came to a tragic close on Sunday, May 17, when Charles "Speed" Holman died as his plane crashed just a few hundred feet in front of horrified spectators. A handsome man, Holman was thirty-three years old when he died.

The writer (ten years old in 1931) and his brother, Harold, were eyewitnesses to the Holman crash. With his home movie camera, Harold took pictures of Holman's spectacular flying just before his fatal crash. Unfortunately, Harold did not capture the actual crash on his film, which now is on deposit in the Nebraska Historical Society.

Charles Holman, the first child of W. Judson and Jane Elizabeth Holman, was born in Minneapolis, Minnesota, on December 27, 1898. Later, two more sons and a daughter were born to his parents. In 1900 the family moved to a small farm near Bloomington, Minnesota.

As a boy, Holman was called Charlie, but acquired the nickname Speed after he quit high school his sophomore year and went to work for a Harley-Davidson motorcycle dealer in Minneapolis. He soon got involved in motorcycle racing, but to conceal his racing from his parents, he used the name Jack Speed.

In 1917, when the United States entered World War I, Charles Holman was nineteen years old. He immediately tried to enlist in the Army Air Service, which was then a branch of the Signal Corps. He was rejected for military service because of a hearing defect, which disqualified him as a pilot; and flat feet, which disqualified him for the infantry.

Like many renowned pilots of the 1930s, Holman got his start in flying during the barnstorming days of the previous decade. In 1919 a pair of brothers, Wilbur and Weldon Larrabee, leased some lands and erected a hangar on the infield portion of an old motor speedway near Fort Snelling, Minnesota. In addition to providing flight training, sightseeing, and charter services, they were sales agents for the Canadian version of the Curtis JN-4 Jenny, called a Canuck. After starting out as a general handyman for the Larrabee brothers in 1919, Charles graduated to wing walking and parachute jumping, using the name Jack Speed.

In the spring of 1920, Speed's father, Judd Holman, was persuaded to attend one of the Sunday afternoon air shows. Unexpectedly, the father got a bigger surprise than he anticipated when Jack Speed dropped to the ground practically at his feet, and he discovered that Speed was his son Charles. In the father-son discussion that followed, Charles agreed to discontinue his wing walking and parachute jumping if Judd would buy Charlie his own airplane. Thus, Charles became the owner of an airplane, a war-surplus Standard J-1, the airplane in which he soloed a short while later.

After several years of barnstorming and flying in air shows, Holman joined Northwest Airways, Inc., which had been formed in 1925 by several St. Paul businessmen. In 1927 Holman became operations manager for the company. The fledgling airline had three Stinson Detroiter planes, in one of which Holman set three Minneapolis-to-Chicago speed records. While flying for Northwest Airways, Holman continued to take part in air shows and air races. On March 17, 1928, over St. Paul, Minnesota, Holman set a new world record for 11,433 consecutive loops, a record that stood for twenty-two years.

In 1930 Holman teamed up with Matty Laird, who had been commissioned by the B.F. Goodrich Rubber Company to build a special racing plane to enter the Thompson Trophy Race, the premier racing event at the National Air Races in Cleveland. Laird finished building the plane, a biplane powered by a 470-horsepower Pratt and Whitney Wasp Junior engine, just days before the scheduled race. Holmes flew the black and gold Laird Speedwing to Chicago's Curtiss-Reynolds Airport north of the city, arriving just in time to have the race number seventy-seven slapped on the fuselage with whitewash and to be flagged to the starting line for the Thompson Race.

Other starters in the 1930 Thompson included Army captain Arthur Page, flying a high-wing Curtis Hawk; Frank Hawks, flying the Texaco sponsored Travel Air Mystery Ship, winner of the 1929 Thompson Race; Benny Howard, flying *Pete*; Jimmy Haizlip, flying another Travel Air Mystery Ship; Harry Williams, flying a Wedell-Williams racer; and Paul Adams, flying a Travel Air Speedwing biplane. The planes were flagged off at ten-second intervals for the one hundred-mile race, which consisted of twenty laps around a five-mile course.

Tragedy struck the race in the seventeenth lap when Arthur Page, while leading, crashed after rounding the home pylon. Carbon monoxide fumes caused Page to black out. He died from his injuries on the following day. With Page out of the race, Holman and Haizlip battled it out, wing to wing, with Holman crossing the finish line just seconds ahead of Haizlip. Benny Howard came in third. Holman in his Laird Solution was the only biplane to win the Thompson Trophy Race. For his win, Holman received five thousand dollars ($34,940 in 2002 prices) which he turned over to Goodyear.

As noted in the previous chapter, Holman flew into Omaha on Saturday afternoon, just in time to enter and win the free-for-all race. On the next day, Sunday, just after Dorothy

Hester broke the women's record for outside loops, Holman raced to his black and gold Laird and got ready for an unscheduled exhibition. After draining all the gasoline, except from the Laird's wing tanks, Don Kelley, Holman's mechanic, began cranking the inertia starter. Holman told Kelley not to leave the crank in place, as he said he was going to fly upside down and did not want it to come loose and hit him in the face.

Jimmy Haizlip, who was in Omaha as an observer, not a participant in the races, reported in an unpublished report he wrote about the Holman crash that the breeze was strong that afternoon, about twenty-five knots, out of the south. For his performance, Holman made an exciting takeoff, holding the Laird tail high as he roared down the runway well past the normal point of liftoff, and then pulling the stick back to climb almost vertically to over one thousand feet before starting his act. Edward Morrow, a reporter for the *Omaha World-Herald*, and Loren Kennedy staff writer for the *Omaha Bee-News*, wrote dramatic eyewitness accounts of the Holman crash.

To this day, there is no clear and final explanation for the Holman crash. Several things seem to be certain, however. It is clear that Holman's body was seen falling halfway out of the cockpit just before the crash. He was not wearing the shoulder harness that had been made available to him by Matty Laird. The belief is that as Holman found himself falling out of the cockpit, he held himself in by thrusting his knees against the inside of the cockpit, which caused him to lose control of the rudder. As the plane veered toward the crowd, it is speculated that he held himself in with the control stick and kicked at the rudder to steer the plane away from the crowd. This last second heroic action pulled the nose of the plane directly toward the ground. Traveling at more than 250 miles per hour, the plane crashed seventy-five feet in front of the Dean Noyes Section. Holman was killed instantly. The air speed indicator read 258 miles per hour. Speed was by no means oblivious to the risks he was taking, for he had been heard to say on one occasion, "Prob-

Witness Paints Vivid Picture of 'Speed' Holman's Death

By LOREN KENNEDY
Bee News Staff Writer

I was the first person to reach the body of Speedy Holman.

Standing against the fence, I watched the black plane catapulting down the field, its pilot leaning from the pit with his head toward the ground.

But something was wrong. He was too close to the ground. Perhaps it was only the fraction of a second—I couldn't tell—but it seemed hours that the ship roared into the center of the field almost scraping the ground.

Then it happened.

The plane was grinding into the oiled surface of the field. It bounced and, crumpling back onto the field, seemed to raise a cloud of dust and debris that floated into the air like the recording of a slow motion picture.

DUST CLEARS AWAY

I shouted and started to run across the field. Other people were screaming and running forms appeared from every direction. Some figures inside the field fence seemed to be racing toward the stands, ordering the crowds to keep their seats. The wreckage was folding into a heap. The dust was clearing away.

Suddenly I stood in the middle of a mass of wreckage, twisted rods and torn canvas and 10 feet away from the smoking pile of junk lay a broken, torn body.

"Speed" Holman had been hurled onto his back, with his face turned skyward and his parachute ropes clinging to his leather belt, holding the motionless body to the motor wreckage in which they were tangled.

CALM FACE, EYES CLOSED

Across the flyers' chest was a bit of torn, black fuselage covering and his legs were bent horribly. One shoe was torn away and his coveralls were stained with dirt and grease. But there was not violence in the upturned face. It was a clam face with closed eyes.

I grasped Holman's wrist from the ground in both hands, trying to find a pulse, but I felt none. Had there been a pulse I wouldn't have known.

Then a feeling of sickness, like a wave against which I had been fighting, overcame me. Other persons were around the wreckage and a mechanic had again picked up Holman's wrist.

Two men were bending over the crushed body. One of them looked up with tears in his eyes, horror written across his face. A third and then a fourth joined them at the flyer's side.

"Steady yourself," a voice was shouting in my ear. I was yanking at the cords that led from a belt around Holman's body into the wreckage. Lieutenant Martin Jensen of the police department grasped the hindering cords beside me.

A man was fumbling with a knife and the lieutenant took it from him. We pulled the ropes taunt, Jensen slashing desperately.

SHEET COVERS BODY

From down the field a siren sounded and an ambulance careened alongside the pile of splintered wood and steel. A fire truck followed, from which men leaped with extinguishers in their hands.

Strong arms raised the wrenched body from the ground as an emergency stretcher bounced out of the ambulance. Then a sheet was drawn over "Speed" Holman. An attendant tucked a limp arm under the covering.

"There isn't going to be any fire," one fireman shouted to his mates.

"Hold back those crowds," pleaded a doctor from the ambulance steps.

"Here's his shoe," called a spectator from the tangled pile.

Nausea spread through the group milling about the plane. Cameras clicked busily amid pleading calls for a clear shot at the wreck.

GIVE HIM A BREAK

And a pilot, dressed in knickers and his face ashen colored, struck wildly at a photographer bent on a picture of the stretcher disappearing into the ambulance.

"He's dead. For God's sake give him a break. You don't need pictures," the pilot screamed.

A band was playing furiously from back in the grandstand, and two automobiles, one a fire truck and the other an ambulance, were clanging noisily for a path through the crowds.

A doctor picked up a small black satchel.

"Holman is dead," he said.

The crowd heard. Then it turned its attention to the wreckage.

"As If Were Cardboard"

Eye-Witness Tells the Story of Speed Holman's Death.

BY EDWARD MORROW.
Eye-Witness of Holman's Crash.

"Speed" Holman in the air, cutting capers. His trim black biplane shrieks over the field, the motor roaring until the din is deafening.

Up, up he goes, two thousand feet. Lazily the biplane turns on its side, drifts down. Then, as the motor thunders again, it gains speed on its downward drive to ward the center of the field.

The spectators gasp as the plane zooms. It seems that the black ship must dive to the center of the earth.

Then, a hundred feet from the ground, the ship "levels off" and Holman skims across the field, a black flash moving 3 hundred miles an hour. Twenty feet from the ground it straightens out, a hundred yards from the tense stands.

Across the field, Holman begins another· of those unbelievable climbs. It seems as if the plane is rushing upward almost vertically at two hundred miles an hour. The people in the stands can hear the wire rigging scream in the wind.

At two thousand feet the ship stalls, slides over on its side. Another wing-over, a barrel loop.

Then, from the north, Holman turns again toward the field, turns the nose of the plane down. Down comes the plane, down down .

About three hundred feet in the air the black plane spins, flops over on its back.

"Seems an Age."

The motor roars ·on, the wires scream .

The plane stays on its back, still headed toward the earth.

Three hundred miles an hour.

At 75 feet the plane begins to level off, still upside down.

The spectators, agonized, wish Holman would abandon this insanity No man should taunt death like that, to give the crowd a thrill.

Still the plane swoops down. The speed is blinding, but to the watchers it seems an age.

Then, at 25 feet, the plane levels off, starts to skim across the field, the landing gear pointing skyward.

The wings wabble, quiver. The motor thunders on.

Then as it seems that Holman may accomplish the impossible, and climb with the plane upside down, it happens.

There is a jerk, the nose points down.

The ship hits the ground, Holman underneath.

There is a tearing crash. The plane folds up before our eyes, as if it were cardboard. Dust fills the air while pieces of wreckage are still flying.

A sheet of metal goes bouncing off to one side as the wreckage settles down.

A thin stream of smoke rises from the motor, where it lies apart from the other wreckage.

There are screams from the stands and women faint. Men say, "God . . ."

Fat policemen, reporters, photographers, officials, a doctor, a priest run toward the· heap of fabric, wires, broken metal.

"Get Him Out!"

Get him out! Get him out!" someone screams.

But there is no need.

Holman's body lies entangled in the wreckage, bound by wires and torn canvas to a heap that two minutes ago was a darting, graceful thing.

An ambulance and a fire truck slide to a stop. The firemen jump off and seize extinguishers, but the wreck is not burning.

Holman's shoes lie ten feet from his body. Strange what one notices.

A half dozen men tread cautiously into the heap and seize the daredevil's smashed body. As if it did any good!

A man rises from those leaning over and shouts, "Who's got a knife? Christ, doesn't somebody have a knife?"

Somebody brings a knife and Holman's body is cut away from the jumble

The body is loaded into the ambulance. Policemen form a ring around the wreck.

The ambulance drives off. A tractor backs up to pull away the wreckage.

The announcer says, "The next event will be.

The band begins to play.

ably, I'll get it sometime, but when death comes, I'll do a thorough job of it."

Later the wreckage of Holman's plane was burned, and the motor buried. No part was sold for junk, and, as far as is known, no parts of the plane were lost to souvenir hunters. Until the wreckage was taken away, Nebraska National Guard troops surrounded it.

Department of Commerce Air Inspector, J.E. Boudwin, who planned to ground Holman after the flight for performing aerobatics too close to the crowd, said after the crash that a corroded loop of the bracket holding the seat belt to the airframe apparently snapped because of strain of the centrifugal force the plane encountered as it leveled off from its dive from the north. H.N. Peterson, traffic manager for the Boeing Company, and Eddie Stinson, both of whom witnessed the crash, believed that gusty surface winds were the main cause of the crash. At the speed at which Holman was traveling, a strong gust hitting the plane could easily have been the cause for the loss of control.

Jimmy Haizlip, a fellow race pilot and eyewitness to the crash, later speculated that Holman might have forgotten to adjust the airplane's trim before his final dive. As Haizlip said,

> Did he remember to trim his aircraft tail heavy? That is a *must* if you have been flying a high power in a normal position. It keeps the nose up and corrects any tendency to dive in case an elevator control slipped. Conversely, when inverted, the nose-high setting tries to make the airplane dive. Added to this, an efficient high-lift wing, so desirable for normal flight, joins hands with gravity and then that old pilot's enemy (i.e., gravity) becomes a welcome helper. It still offers lift, but downward instead of up.

Haizlip went on to say that in checking later with some of the line mechanics who saw the crash, their impression was that in Holman's "...struggle to hold the airplane's nose up in that

44

first abortive, inverted dive, his tremendous strength broke his lap belt."

When a telegraph operator reached Holman's wife, Dee, at the Holman's home in Minneapolis, she refused to take the message, telling her sister, "I know Charlie's been killed, will you take the message." When news of Holman's death reached Northwest Airways, several officials of the company, members of the St. Paul Aero Club, and other dignitaries flew to Omaha to accompany Holman's body by train back to the Twin Cities. The body was taken to a funeral home in Minneapolis, where it lay in state until the funeral services on May 21. It was estimated that more than one hundred thousand people attended Holman's funeral, watched the funeral procession, or came to the grave side. Speed was buried in Acacia Park Cemetery in Mendota Heights, Minnesota at a spot that Holman himself had selected. As his casket was lowered into the ground, a formation of US Navy planes in a broken V formation flew over, along with twenty-one civilian planes from the Minneapolis and St. Paul airports.

As my brother and I returned to our Florence Boulevard home after the races, newsboys were on the streets calling out, "Extras! Extra! Holman killed in crash." There was no television then, and even radio was still somewhat primitive. So when there was a major news story, the newspapers got out extra editions, usually sold by newsboys hawking them in the streets. Big, black headlines were always a standard feature of extras.

In an editorial, the *New York World Telegram* said:

> They buried Speed Holman on the highest point between Minneapolis and Chicago, along the route of Northwest Airways, where he can forever keep an invisible charge over the great airline system that he loved and managed so well. He ran his airline safely and sanely. He was a credit to the company for which he worked. But he was wild and wooly when he sat in his own personal airplane.

45

Holman died as Rockne (Notre Dame football coach, Knute Rockne, who was killed in an airplane crash) died, at the peak of his career. He died as he lived, with a roar and a flash at three hundred miles per hour.

In 1932 the St. Paul Municipal Airport was renamed Holman Field, and a seven-ton granite block with a bronze tablet memorializing Holman was placed at the entrance to the airport.

4

Four Days of Racing

maha's second annual air races began in 1932 on May 27—a sunny Friday afternoon—after dozens of racing pilots and their airplanes had streamed into the city for the air meet. An extra feature that year was the start of the national balloon races, the winner of which would become the United States entry in the Gordon Bennett International Balloon Races in Switzerland in September.

Earl Ortman from San Francisco was the first to arrive on Thursday, towing the fuselage of his plane, *Miss San Francisco*, a Keith Ryder special, on a trailer. Ortman was accompanied by Bud Pearson, one of the builders of the plane. When the wings arrived by express, Ortman and Pearson assembled the plane. With just 250 hours of flight time, the twenty-year-old Ortman was making his debut as a racing pilot. Next to arrive were the Hollywood Hawks, Roy Wilson and Frank Clarke, the famed aerobatic team that had provided the stunts for almost every air movie ever made. They came in two Travelair Speedwing planes.

Betty Lund, whose husband Freddy Lund was killed in a crash in Council Bluffs a few weeks after the 1931 races, arrived with her German shepherd, *Spin*, who had about a thousand fly-

Above: William Ong.

At left: Stub Quinby and Johnny Livingston.

ing hours to his credit. Art Davis and his wife, Rhoda, also a pi-
lot, flew in their taper-wing Wacos from East Lansing,
Michigan. Davis had won a free-for-all race the year before at
Omaha in one of the Wacos.

Late in the afternoon, Benny Howard in his all-white,
low-wing *Mike*, with the racing number seven on its side, arrived
flying across the field at about 175 miles per hour, and then
landed to the north. As he started to taxi toward the hangars,
Mike slipped off the runway and got mired down in the mud. As
Howard tried to tug the plane back to drier ground, the plane
was upended and the propeller bent. Happily, Howard was able
to have the propeller transported on an American Airways
plane that was just leaving for Kansas City. The propeller was
straightened there and brought back to Omaha by noon on Friday.

Another pilot, who had been at Omaha in 1931, was
Johnny Livingston of Aurora, Illinois, who arrived in his
clipped-wing Monocoupe, which he claimed
could do 190 miles per hour. The plane was
called clipped-wing because Livingston re-
placed the original wings with ones that were
nine feet shorter. Livingston planned to both
race and compete in the aerobatic contests.
Another well-known pilot among the thirty
entrants for the races was Steve Wittman of
Oshkosh, Wisconsin, who arrived in his
mid-wing monoplane, *Chief Oshkosh*, in
which he had taken two first places at the
Miami Air Races earlier in January.

Steve Wittman

The Friday Races

After the opening ceremonies, the first event of the 1932
races was the dead-stick landing contest. W.W. Kranz of Louisville, Kentucky, won this event, which required the pilot to cut
his engine at an altitude of fifteen hundred feet, and then land

2 Women Fliers Arrive for Air Race Meet

Mrs. Art Davis   Herbert Elkins   Betty Lund

as close as possible to the center of a target. He landed just seven feet from the target. Cliff Kysor of Ottumwa, Iowa, was second at nine feet, three and one-half inches from the center; and Marcellus King from Fairmont, Minnesota, third, at eleven feet, seven inches.

In the Sportsman Pilot Race, the first race of the day, Dr. John D. Brock of Kansas City, the "Flying Optician," took first place. Dr. Brock who had also won the Sportsman Pilot Race in 1931 held the world's record for consecutive daily flights. Second place went to William Warrick of Cleveland, Ohio, and third to Cliff Henderson, also from Cleveland and manager of the Cleveland National Air Races. The Sportsman Pilots Race

Auto-giro at Omaha Air Races on Saturday.
First to be flown west of the Mississippi River.

was open only to planes of less than five hundred cubic inches of displacement.

Following the Sportsman Pilot Race, Betty Lund put on a dazzling display of aerobatics, doing loops, three double snap rolls, and inverted figure eights. She concluded by flying her plane upside down across the field in front of the grandstand, a maneuver that reminded spectators of Speed Holman's ill-fated final dive at the 1931 races.

By the time the parachute jumping contest got under way after Betty Lund's performance, the wind had picked up sharply, which made for difficult jumps, none of which approached normal accuracy. First place in the parachute jumping contest went to Clem Sohn of Lansing, Michigan, who landed 120 feet from the center of the ring. Second was Dick Hunter of Minneapolis, Minnesota, who landed 250 feet away, while Jerry Wessling of Toledo, Ohio, took third, landing 600 feet from the target. Roger Don Rae of Lansing, Michigan, who had won more parachute jumps than any other American jumper, failed to place.

The novelty Pony Express Race, won by Johnny Livingston of Aurora, Illinois, was a crowd pleaser. In this race, the fliers circled the five-mile course three times. After a racehorse start and at the end of the first lap, they had to land and drink a bottle of milk. Then, at the end of the second lap, they landed again to eat a sandwich and drink a bottle of pop. On the third lap, they flew over the finish line. Second place went to Cliff Kysor of Ottumwa, Iowa, and third place to Eldon Cessna of Wichita, Kansas. In all, seven planes entered the race.

About mid-afternoon, a squadron of seven Army Boeing P-12 pursuit planes belonging to the 430th Squadron from the Heart of the Nation Reserve Corps at Kansas City flew over the field and then landed. Commanded by Captain William B. Wright, the planes took off shortly thereafter and executed many formation maneuvers, while concluding their show with a simulated strafing of the airport. Later in the afternoon three Navy Curtis Helldivers, led by Lieutenant Frank E. Weld, flew in from the Naval reserve air station in St. Louis. As in 1931, an auto-giro was present, and was still enough of a novelty to draw the crowd's attention. This year the auto-giro came from Willow Springs, Pennsylvania, and was flown by Jimmy Faulkner, who put the craft through the usual maneuvers, sideways and backwards flying, steep banks and climbs, motionless hovering, and near vertical takeoffs and landings.

In the feature ATC (Approved Type Certificate) Race, in which pure racing planes are ineligible, George F. Harte of Wichita, Kansas, took first place, followed by George Shealy from Wichita, Kansas, who took second place. Art Davis of Lansing, Michigan, was leading the race for three laps when a broken valve in his motor forced him out, making a dead-stick landing necessary. After he landed, Davis said, "A valve went bad and I had to cut the motor, or it would have torn things up. I was picking a good cornfield on the river bank for a landing, but I managed to turn and make port. I wasn't in much trouble."

In the free-for-all race for planes with motors of not over a 275 cubic inch displacement, Harold Neumann in a Monocoupe took first place, followed by Art Chester in a Davis Sport, John Starr in a Baby Ace, and W.W. Kranz in an Aeronca C-3, who with a comic touch, floated his tiny plane sideways across the finish line.

Late in the afternoon and to wrap up the first day's program, the Hollywood Hawks put on their dazzling exhibition of aerobatic flying doing spins, snap rolls, slow rolls, Immelmans, wingovers, inside and outside loops, and concluding with a simulated dogfight just as it is done in the movies. They each landed in spectacular fashion, coming out of a low-level loop to touch down and end the act.

The Saturday Races

In the fastest time yet for the Omaha Air Races, Robert Clampett, a San Francisco broker flying the Keith Ryder Special, *Miss San Francisco*, nosed out Benny Howard in *Mike* by a scant twenty-five feet to take first place in the five hundred cubic inch free-for-all race on Saturday. The race was twenty-five miles, and Clampett won it with an average speed of 176.06 miles per hour, just slightly faster than Howard's average of 175.84 miles per hour. For first place, Clampett won $270 and Howard received $150 for second.

53

Johnny Livingston, who came in fourth in his clipped-wing Monocoupe, took the lead momentarily as the planes took off in the racehorse start, but both Clampett and Howard passed Livingston on the backstretch of the course. Howard almost took the lead away from Clampett on the fourth lap, but the prop wash from Clampett's plane pushed Howard's racer out from the pylon, and Howard never made up the distance. Both Clampett and Howard reached speeds of 200 miles per hour on the straightaways, and 190 miles per hour on the pylon turns. Herman Hammer of LaSalle, Illinois, came in third with an average speed of 170.44 miles per hour, Johnny Livingston fourth at 169.44 miles per hour, and Steve Wittman fifth at 162.84 miles per hour.

Saturday's program began with a model airplane contest, in which eighty-five boys were entered. The winner of the junior duration flight was Omaha resident Jack Furstenberg, whose model stayed aloft for one minute, fifty-one and one-half seconds. Charles Carey, also of Omaha, won the free-for-all, and Marven Pehrson of Red Oak, Iowa, came in first in the Pony Express Senior division. The five top winners received airplane rides.

In Saturday's Pony Express Race, the format was changed. Instead of landing to eat a sandwich or drink a glass of milk or bottle of pop, lines were painted on the runway in front of the grandstand. Each pilot had to stop his plane, throttle it down, and jump out of the cockpit to shake hands with a man stationed there. Art Davis came in first, followed by Cliff Kysor, second; and George Shealy, third. Roger Don Rae, who jumped from twenty-five hundred feet and landed just three feet, seven inches from the target, won the parachute jump on Saturday. His prize was forty-five dollars. To close the Saturday program, four parachutists jumped from a cabin plane, following a wing-walking and rope-ladder hanging exhibit by Fiddle Miller of Clarinda, Iowa, in the same plane.

The Sunday Races

More than twenty thousand persons witnessed the Sunday races, setting a new attendance record, which exceeded by one-third the maximum attendance at any of the previous years' races. Besides those in paid attendance, hundreds more watched the races from open fields around the airport. The *Omaha Bee-News* reported the fields between the east boundary of the airport and the Missouri River were "black with cars."

For Sunday's program the focus of attention was on the unlimited free-for-all. Russell Boardman of Cape Code, Massachusetts, won the race with an average speed of 176.69 miles per hour. Benny Howard came in second with an average speed of 175.54 miles per hour, followed by Earl Ortman in *Miss San Francisco* with an average speed of 174.28 miles per hour. In winning the free-for-all, Boardman set a new Omaha meet speed record, surpassing the record Robert Clampett had set on Saturday.

Boardman took the lead from the start of the race, never relinquishing it, although Ortman held second place for three laps, close behind Boardman. At the first turn on the first lap, Howard was in fifth place, but he gradually crept up on the leaders, passing Ortman on the fourth lap to finish in second place. The other racers in the order they finished were Johnny Livingston, Roy Liggett, Art Davis, Steve Wittman, and Karl Martin. Prize money went to Boardman, $360; Howard, $200; Livingston, $80; and Liggett, $40.

On a whimsical note later in the afternoon, Russell Boardman was made an honorary member of the Grand Island Whisker Club. Organized to commemorate the seventy-fifth anniversary of Hall County, where Grand Island is located. Members of the club flew into Omaha early in the afternoon in five aircraft, which flew over the field in a V-formation before landing. Boardman, who held the world's long distance championship for his flight from New York to Istanbul, Turkey, in the summer of 1931, reportedly enthusiastically accepted the award even though clean shaven, he wore a sixteen-inch false beard tied around his chin.

The record-breaking crowd experienced a tense moment during the parachute jumping contest. After Dick Hunter of Minneapolis bailed out at three thousand feet, he became entangled in the cloth of his main chute, falling, perhaps three hundred feet before the pilot chute pulled him free and his main chute opened fully. Hunter won second place in the contest, landing eighty feet away from the target. Roger Don Rae of Lansing, Michigan, Saturday's winner, was again the winner on Sunday, landing forty-eight feet from the target.

Again, the Hollywood Hawks—Roy Wilson and Frank Clark—put on a dazzling display of aerobatics, commencing several thousand feet above the ground and ending with a spectacular dogfight that took them at times to an altitude of just a few hundred feet high in front of the stands. As usual, they turned on the smoke, leaving a trail of their intricate maneuvers in the cloudless sky. After their act, they expressed regret that Department of Commerce regulations prevented them from showing "all our stunts… We have a contract to make an air picture when the show is over," Clark said, "and we cannot afford to lose our licenses."

Twenty-eight planes were entered in the dead-stick landing contest, which was won by W.W. Krantz of Louisville, Kentucky, who had also won this contest on Friday and placed third on Saturday. He put his tiny Aeronca down just eight feet, seven inches from the target. Second place went to Ray Schenck of Clarinda, Iowa, who hit nine feet, eleven inches from the mark, while Harold Neumann was third at ten feet, eight inches away.

In other Sunday races, Johnny Livingston won the Waco Race at an average speed of 103.11 miles per hour, followed by Tex La Grone, who crowded Livingston all the way to the finish, nearly catching Livingston on the straight-aways, but falling behind on the pylon turns. Art Davis came in third in the Waco Race. In the manufacturer's race for Monocoupes, Marcellus

King of Fairmont, Minnesota, took first place; followed by Harold Neumann with second; and Jerry Nettleton of Toledo, Ohio, with third.

Monday, the Final Day of Racing

In a thrilling last minute finish, Benny Howard in *Mike* nosed out Russell Boardman in his Gee Bee Y to win the twenty-five mile free-for-all that closed out the 1932 Omaha air races. Howard's average speed was 179.96 miles per hour, the fastest in the four-day meet, while Boardman averaged 179.06 miles per hour.

Boardman led for the first four laps, but on the last pylon turn, Howard pulled up and over Boardman. After the race, Boardman said, "I gave it everything I could under the weather conditions, but Howard's pylon turns were superb." There was rain in the morning, but it ended before the races began. The winds continued strong, which Howard said made for a tough ride. "Boardman was hard to beat," he added.

Near disaster overtook Earl Ortman flying *Miss San Francisco* in the race. While rounding the north pylon on the second lap of the race, the wind whipped his goggles from his head. Half-blinded by oil shooting into his face from the engine, Ortman scraped the trees but managed to stay in the race, taking wide turns on the pylons. Johnny Livingston passed him on the next lap to finish third, but Ortman managed to stay in the race and finish fourth. Behind him came Roy Liggett to finish fifth, and Art Davis, sixth. When Ortman landed, he discovered one wing had been perforated where it brushed the trees. Asked if he was scared when he brushed the trees, Ortman replied, "Scared? You don't have time to be scared at that speed." For first place money, Howard collected one thousand dollars, the largest purse for any of the 1932 races.

In the Sportsman Pilot Race, Harry Sidles of Lincoln, Nebraska, took first place; followed by Cliff Henderson of Cleveland took second; and William Warrick, also of Cleveland, took third. The first forced landing off the airport came during the ATC Race when the motor on A.A. Krantz's Aeronca quit because of a blown cylinder. He was forced to land in a field midway between the second pylon and the home pylon. Krantz was not injured. This race was won by Harold Neumann, followed by Art Chester of Joliet, Illinois, and William Reedholm of Boxholm, Iowa.

Because of the gusty winds, the parachute jumping contest turned out to be especially thrilling. Roger Don Rae won the jump at a distance of 377 feet from the target, and Jerry Wessling of Toledo, Ohio, was second at 417 feet. The excitement came when one jumper landed in the automobile parking south of the airport, another on the north boundary of the airport, and a third barely missed planes lined up for the Pony Express Race. The Pony Express Race was won by Johnny Livingston with Eldon Cessna, second; and Marcellus King, third.

G.R. Lockhart, the first Omahan to win a major event at the races, won the dead-stick landing contest. He put his plane down two feet, six inches from the mark, closely followed by Bill Reedholm of Boxholm, Iowa, whose distance was three feet, six inches. Third place went to Eldon Cessna of Wichita at a distant fifteen feet, eight inches. Twenty planes entered this event.

In the Speed Holman Aerobatics Contest, Russell Boardman, in thirty minutes of aerial stunting in his Gee Bee Y, won the cup from the Hollywood Hawks, although Roy Wilson told the *Omaha World-Herald* that he and his partner intended to protest the award. No action was ever taken on the protest, the only one registered during the races.

The paper, in describing Boardman's performance, said:

> He zoomed his plane immediately after take-off; climbed straight up until his engine sputtered and stalled; dropped earthward out of control, spiraling crazily like a leaf in a storm; recovered to go into a series of loops and spins, flying for a time upside

down; climbed above the clouds and shot toward earth like a shot of lightning; and ended with a series of maneuvers close to the ground. Several times it appeared to the spectators that the plane had touched the ground.

Rain that lasted throughout the morning and threatened again during the afternoon cut attendance to about six thousand, half the size of the Sunday crowd. This turned the 1932 races into a losing venture for the Omaha Junior Chamber of Commerce.

5

The Balloon Races

On Sunday afternoon on May 29, 1932, the day before the balloon races were to start, Captain W. J. Flood of Washington, D.C., and pilot of the Army's Balloon Number 1 said he was happy to see the weather forecast indicating that a storm was headed for the Omaha area.

"We don't want to fly in a storm," he hastened to explain, "but if we can get a storm fifty to one hundred miles away from Omaha and take off ahead of it, conditions will perfect." What the balloonists want is to be shoved ahead by the storm.

Six balloons were successfully launched that Monday evening from Omaha's Municipal Airport before an estimated six thousand spectators who remained after the air races to see the balloons take to the air. Two balloons narrowly escaped disaster but did manage to take off. The first balloon rose at 6:50 in the evening, and the last, the *City of Omaha*, finally got away after a balky start at 8:47.

The six balloons took off in the following order:

Chevrolet at 6:50 P.M.
United States Army Number 1 at 7:17 P.M.
United States Army Number 2 at 7:44 P.M.
City of Detroit at 8:10 P.M.

Goodyear at 8:24 P.M.
City of Omaha at 8:47 P.M.

The first excitement came on the initial takeoffs, when the twenty-three mile per hour wind carried *Chevrolet* north along the runway to a fence and knocked it down before bouncing along across the marshy lands north of the airport. Pilot Tracy Southworth and his copilot John E. Eagle, both members of the Detroit Balloon Club, threw overboard several sacks of ballast as the balloon approached the fence, but it still did not rise. After knocking down the fence, and the pilots tossing out still more ballast, the balloon finally rose, narrowly missing the trees.

"It looks more like a steeplechase than a balloon race," one spectator observed.

This precarious takeoff was almost exactly duplicated by Army Balloon Number 2, piloted by Lieutenant W.J. Paul with Sergeant John Bishop as copilot. It, too, skimmed along the runway, then barely cleared the fence as Paul and Bishop tossed out ballast. It bounced along over the pasture, and then finally rose just before reaching the tress. As with *Chevrolet*, the winds then carried the balloon to the northwest.

Army Balloon Number 1, commanded by Captain W.J. Flood of Washington, D.C., made a successful, almost vertical takeoff, and then followed *Chevrolet* aloft to the northwest in the estimated forty mile per hour winds. This balloon was equipped with liquid oxygen, which would permit it to fly as high as twenty-six thousand feet. Captain Flood said before takeoff that he hoped his balloon would reach New England.

Weather maps available at the time of the launching indicated that the winds would drive the balloons to the northeast over the Great Lakes where they would pick up northwesterly winds that would drive them into the eastern section of the United States.

The first balloon to get in trouble was the *City of Detroit*. Piloted by Pete and Harold Larsen, the *City of Detroit* never gained enough altitude and after a bare ten minutes of flying, it landed on an island in the Missouri River near Fort Calhoun, Nebraska. Neither the pilots nor the balloon suffered any injuries or damage.

The *Chevrolet* entry made it through the night, but after a wild ride through electrical storms and snow, it came down about four miles from Jamestown, North Dakota, at 8:15 Tuesday morning. It had flown 410 miles. The balloon's captain, Tracy W. Southworth, who was also a member of the Michigan Legislature, told the *Omaha Bee-News* via telephone that he and his copilot, John E. Engle of Detroit, had some "pretty rough flying." Continuing, he said:

> We took off with less ballast than we should have because of conditions at Omaha. We shot up to 10,000 feet and ran into an electrical storm.
>
> The atmosphere was charged. The damp ropes around the balloon were charged with static electricity. The lightning was flying all around us. We dumped overboard all the ballast that we dared, but still could not rise above the storm, so we let out some gas and got below the storm.
>
> For about two and one-half hours we flew along on our drag rope. It was over South Dakota, I guess. The wind was strong, and we were rambling along. We had only two bags of ballast left.
>
> This morning we shot up to 12,500 feet, but we were still in the clouds and it was snowing. Before long we were down on the drag rope again, and for an hour we scuttled over the North Dakota landscape. Our drag rope went through some fences and telephone lines, and then we saw we were heading right into a high tension line. We dumped everything overboard, even our spare clothing, to let the basket up so it would miss the power line. And we came down in a field.

The fields are big up here in North Dakota. The wind was 35 miles an hour and it was raining. We opened the values, but the basket was dragged over the ground for another 400 feet before the gas was out."

Southward went on to say that it was one of the fastest balloon rides he had ever taken, especially while not flying high. The point where they landed was 410 miles from Omaha. They came in fifth in the race.

The next balloon to come down was the *City of Omaha*, which had a rough landing near McKenzie, North Dakota, which is 450 miles north of Omaha. Pilot E.J. Hill and the copilot Roscoe G. Conklin, both of Omaha, were slightly injured in the landing. Conklin suffered a sprained ankle and Hill a cut over the eye when they were spilled from the basket after the balloon struck a fence. They were in the air fourteen hours. Conklin said,

Oh what a ride. It was terrible all the way. There was an electrical storm and rain every moment. We got up to six thousand feet, and there was so much lightning we had to duck and get under. Then this morning we went back up for a while again, and the rain got worse.

And how we came down! Hard: like a ton of bricks.

We were coming down for two miles. We missed some wires and things, dragged across a river that was a regular torrent, missed a branch, and smashed into a fence. I pulled the valve and Hill pulled the rip cord, and there we were, all piled up in a heap... I either broke my ankle or sprained it, and Hill's got a bad eye cut and another cut on the face. And there's such a downpour it was all the truck could do to get us to Bismarck.

Army Balloon Number *1* landed at 12:30 in the afternoon Tuesday near Sherwood, North Dakota, about three miles from the Canadian border. This spot is about 607 miles from Omaha, and on Tuesday afternoon it was the greatest distance from Omaha yet reported by any of the four balloons. At the time Army Balloon Number *1* came down, the exact whereabouts of the other two balloons still in the race—Army Balloon Number *2* and *Goodyear*—were unknown. The balloon's captain, W.J. Flood, said the trip had been rough because of the stormy weather. Lieutenant Haymie McCormick, copilot, said the balloon climbed to twelve thousand feet in an attempt to escape the storm, but was unable to avoid it. Flood and McCormick became exhausted from fighting the storm and decided to land. In landing, the balloon struck a high-tension line before touching down, but trees broke its fall, and neither Flood nor McCormick was injured. After landing, Flood and McCormick dismantled the balloon and made plans to leave on Wednesday for Omaha.

The second place winner in the race, the *Goodyear*, piloted by R. J. Blair and F. A. Trotter, came down at Tyvan, Saskatchewan, 710 miles from Omaha. The *Goodyear* crew reported they were fired upon by a farmer with a high-powered rifle as they passed over a corner of Manitoba. After fighting lightning, thunder, and rain through Nebraska, South Dakota, and North Dakota, they ran into snow as they entered Canada.

In a telegram to the *Omaha Bee-News*, Blair and Trotter said "…we made the fastest landing from a free balloon ever attempted."

Army Number *2* won the race, landing at 1:00 in the morning on Wednesday, thirteen miles north of Hatton, Saskatchewan, Canada, 901 miles northwest of Omaha. Army Number *2* was in the air twenty-nine hours. In their flight, balloon pilot Lieutenant W. J. Paul and copilot Sergeant John Bishop broke two world records. The record flight was confirmed by the National Aeronautical Association.

They shattered the prior world duration record for balloons of thirty-five thousand cubic feet capacity—twenty-six hours and forty-six minutes—by staying aloft twenty-nine hours. They also broke the previous world distance record of 571 miles by 330 miles. By winning this race, Army Balloon Number 2 became the United States entry in the international balloon races held in Switzerland.

Lieutenant Paul and Sergeant Bishop also won the Litchfield Trophy donated by P. W. Litchfield, president of the Goodyear Tire and Rubber Company.

Since 1911, when Goodyear designed the first free balloon for the government, the company has built more than eleven hundred free balloons and about 130 airships (powered lighter-than-air craft, also known as dirigibles or Zeppelins). Zeppelins were named for Count Ferdinand von Zeppelin, designer and builder of many famous German airships, including the famed Hindenberg, which crashed and burned at Lakehurst, New Jersey, in 1938, effectively ending transatlantic passenger service by airship.

The landing point for Army Number 2 was almost on the boundary between the provinces of Alberta and Saskatchewan, about eighty-five miles north of the United States border. Paul and Bishop reported that they came down when they reached the center of the storm that carried them from Omaha to the north and northwest. If they had remained aloft, they would have been carried back toward Omaha, thus reducing their chances for a distance record.

Late in the afternoon, Army Balloon Number 2, at about two hundred feet, passed over the town of Woodrow, Saskatchewan, where the crew called out to Wilbur Sampson, a farmer, "What state are we in?" "Saskatchewan," the farmer replied. Later, near the town of Gull Lake, the balloon dropped low enough for some of the residents to grab hold of the drag rope they tossed over from the basket. "Are we near Regina?" Paul and Bishop called out. They were told they were 185 miles west of Regina, the capital of Saskatchewan, after which the balloon was cast loose, picked up altitude, and disappeared from view.

Wallace C. Peterson

With the landing of Army Balloon Number 2, Omaha's 1932 air races came to an end.

6

The Final Air Races

Omaha's final air races were held in 1933 and 1934. In 1933 races were held on three days, June 16, 17, and 18, but in 1934 they were reduced to just two days, August 11 and 12. As usual, the racing planes and their pilots began arriving in Omaha for the 1933 races on Thursday, June 15, the day before Omaha's races began.

One racing plane that attracted much attention was a new, high-wing Cessna monoplane, flown by Johnny Livingston, well-known from previous races in which he flew his clipped-wing Monocoupes. Livingston's plane, a Cessna CR-3 Racer, painted a bright red and yellow, had a 150-horsepower motor, a closed cockpit, and landing gears that retracted into the stubby fuselage just behind the big, radial engine.

Livingston flew his new plane in from Wichita, Kansas, at an average speed of 203 miles per hour. After landing, he said he did not know how fast the plane would really fly, but promised in the race he would open the throttle wide to see.

Among other arrivals were Betty Lund, who had put on dazzling displays of aerobatics in the 1932 races; Frank Faulkner of Willow Grove, Pennsylvania, with his auto-giro; Bob Moore, in a reproduction of a 1910 Curtis Pusher and George Burrell of

Chicago, Illinois, with a Ford Trimotor, in which he planned to do practically all the aerobatics usually done by smaller, single engine airplanes. Charles Abel from Chicago towed his glider, the only biplane glider in the country, to Omaha by automobile. He planned to try to set a new record for consecutive loops in a glider. The record stood at seventeen in 1933.

The Races Begin

Omaha's third annual air races began with the largest opening day crowd since the races started two years earlier. After the air show opened with a model airplane contest, Bennett Griffin put on an aerobatic display as a bomb exploded high in the air, releasing an American flag that floated down under a parachute. A balloon busting and ribbon cutting exhibition immediately followed this by Art Davis.

Next on the program was an exhibition of high speed aerobatics by Johnny Livingston, flying—not his new Cessna racer—but Benny Howard's *Ike,* sister airplane to the Howard *Mike,* a big winner in the 1932 Omaha races. After putting the little Howard racer through thirteen quick barrel rolls, Livingston dived toward the ground from over three thousand feet, attaining a speed in excess of two hundred miles per hour as he swept past the grandstand. Livingston did not, however, attempt to duplicate Charles "Speed" Holman's ill-fated, upside down flight from two years earlier. Further, he stayed farther from the crowd than Holman had.

Both the auto-giro and the Ford Trimotor aerobatics exhibitions were crowd pleasers. Frank Faulkner in the auto-giro demonstrated the climbs, dives, and turns the ungainly craft could make, landing without the use of his motor, and allowing the rotor blades to lower him to a soft landing at about the rate of fifteen feet per second. In the Ford Trimotor, George Burrell did loops, dives, split-S turns, a barrel roll, and a spectacular falling leaf, a maneuver in which the airplane drops aimlessly, seemingly out of total control. In just before landing, Burrell flew across the field in front of the spectators on one wheel and with a wing tip almost dragging the ground. It was a masterful performance.

Comic relief was provided by Dick Granere of Chicago, who, dressed as a farmer with fake whiskers, flew his tiny Aeronca in a crazy fashion back and forth in front of the grandstand, cutting his motor at one point and shouting to the crowd, "How do you get this durn thing down?" Bob Moore, in the 1911 Pusher replica called *Goofus*, sitting out in the open, swooped back and forth across the field, waving to the crowd.

Another spectacular feature of the Friday program was the delayed parachute drop by Clem Sohn, who, stepping out of Art Davis' Waco at eight thousand feet with a twenty-four pound sack of flour, twisted and turned for thousands of feet before pulling his ripcord to open his chute at fifteen hundred feet. The flour traced his path toward the ground for the thousands of enthralled spectators.

On Friday afternoon there was only one race, won by Art Davis of East Lansing, Michigan, in his taper-wing Waco. Second place was claimed by Bennett Griffin, who flew a Travel Air Speedwing. Harold Neuman came in third in another Waco. It was a close race, with Davis taking the lead, then Griffin wresting it away from him on the third lap, and then Davis regaining the lead on the fourth lap and winning the twenty-five-mile race on the final lap by the length of his plane's fuselage.

In the model plane contest, Miles Spickler, age nineteen, took first place with a flight of two minutes and thirteen seconds with his rubber-powered plane that weighed only two ounces. Second place went to Gerald Jensen, with a flight of one minute and thirty-nine seconds, and third place went to Jean Rohife.

Friday's program closed with a demonstration of formation flying by seven planes from the 413th Army Pursuit Squadron stationed at Kansas City. They wound up their act with a simulated "strafing" of the airport.

The Saturday and Sunday Races

In a twenty-mile closed course race, Johnny Livingston defeated Harold Neumann by a sixth of a mile, flying at an average speed of 225 miles per hour. Livingston was flying his new Cessna racer with the retractable landing gear, and Neumann was in Benny Howard's *Ike*.

Initially, Neumann took the lead as Livingston did not crank his Cessna up to full speed while drawing up his retractable landing gear, but on the second lap Livingston caught up with Neumann on the second pylon turn, passed him, and thereafter, never lost the lead. After the race, Livingston said he did not open his plane to full throttle, as he did not want its top speed to be known until after the Chicago Races later in the year. Even so, Livingston's speed was approximately twenty-five miles an hour faster than any speed yet seen at Omaha. For his part, Neumann said he was beaten because the spark on the Howard racer jammed, so that he could not turn on both magnetos.

In the second pylon race of the afternoon, Art Davis repeated his Friday victory over Bennett Griffin, who again came in second, and Harold Neumann, who came in third. As in the Friday race, Neuman took the lead, getting off the ground first. But on the third lap, Davis passed both Griffin and Neumann, winning by a margin of about thirty yards.

A double, delayed action parachute jump by Clem Sohn and Wayne "Mile High" Wagner provided a special thrill for the crowd in the face of strong winds out of the south. Because of the winds, the two jumpers, in planes piloted by Art Davis and L.D. "Dutch" Miller, went to only eight thousand feet, with Wagner stepping off into space first, followed closely by Sohn. Again, the sacks of flour they carried traced the paths of the jumpers out. Both jumpers opened their chutes when about one thousand feet above the ground.

Other events on Saturday included aerobatics by Betty Lund, more antics by Bob Moore in *Goofus*, made more exciting (and hazardous) by the high winds. Also was a display of drunken flying by Frankie Faulkner in the auto-giro, in which he flew backwards and sideways, turned on a dime, and concluded with a perpendicular landing.

The crowd in attendance on Saturday was estimated at ten thousand.

Sunday, the third and last day of Omaha's third annual air races, was almost a carbon copy of Saturday's races. In the showdown race, Johnny Livingston of Aurora, Illinois, once more defeated Harold Neumann. Livingston again flew his red and yellow Cessna, while Neumann was in the all-white Howard *Ike*. As in Saturday's race, Neumann jumped into the lead as the race started, holding it for most of the first lap, but Livingston overtook him on the backstretch of the second lap. For the rest of the race, Livingston held a narrow lead, nosing Neumann out by fifty yards at the finish line.

A near mishap occurred in the delayed action parachute jump when Wayne "Mile High" Wagner jumped from seven thousand feet but didn't open his chute until just five hundred feet above the ground. Apparently his first chute had become entangled, but at five hundred feet his second chute burst from its pack, preventing a tragedy, but resulting in a broken ankle-bone when he hit the ground in a hard landing. Later, he said he had never before come within five hundred feet of the ground before pulling the ripcord on his reserve chute.

At the close of the races on Sunday, Crawford Follmer, manager of the air show, said receipts for the air races would total approximately $11,500 ($270,810 in 2002 prices). An estimated crowd of fifteen thousand, including those who watched from nearby points of vantage, witnessed the last day of the races. Follmer said that the receipts would pay all the expenses but not leave much of a surplus.

The 1934 Races

Omaha's last air races were held on only two days, August 11 and 12 of 1934. Among the arrivals on Friday were Gordon Israel of St. Louis, Missouri, at age twenty-three, one of the youngest professional racing pilots in America; Roger Don Rae from Bryon, Wisconsin, veteran of the Omaha and other air races; Art Chester, from Glenville, Illinois, another leading figure among air race pilots; and Miles Burcham of Muncie, Indiana, a leading aerobatics flyer.

The air races opened at 1:30 on Saturday afternoon, and shortly thereafter, Gordon Israel in his red and white, gull-wing racer, *Redhead*, established a new speed record for Omaha when he roared around the pylons in the qualifying flight for the Eugene Eppley Trophy Race at an average speed of 206.42 miles per hour. This bettered the record set in 1932 by twenty-three miles per hour, and won Israel the pole position for the two thousand dollar, five-mile trophy race on Sunday.

Gordon Israel of Clayton, MO.

Gordon Israel's plane.

Although Israel at the time of the 1934 Omaha air races had only 140 hours in the air, he was one of the nation's leading racing pilots. In the 1933 National Air Races at Cleveland, Israel and *Redhead* took two third place finishes and one fifth, and later in the year at Chicago, he won a second and a third place. With only a high school education, supplemented by some night school classes at Washington University in St. Louis, Israel went to work at the age of twenty-one for Benny Howard, helping him build his famous racer, *Pete*. Israel did the stress analysis for *Pete*, and a year later, he helped in the design and building of Howard's next racer, *Mike*.

Lee Miles of San Bernadino, California, in his Miles and Atwood Special, won first place in the thirty-mile, free-for-all feature race on Saturday for planes with a maximum engine displacement of 375 cubic inches. In the race, Miles reached speeds of 230 miles per hour on the straightaway. Afterwards, he said, "And the ship was throttled down—she's still got some stuff left. I'm out to take Israel tomorrow. He's awful fast, but I may be able to do it."

Miles' prize money was $450 ($5,947 in 2002 prices). Israel could not enter this race because of the size of *Redhead*'s motor. Miles covered the course at an average speed of 196.42 miles per hour, crossing the finish line just ahead of Art Chester, who averaged 194.2 miles per hour in his mid-wing, green and white *Jeep*. Third place went to Steve Wittman of Oshkosh, Wisconsin, flying his *Chief Oshkosh* at an average speed of 191.89 miles per hour, and fourth place went to Joe Jacobson of Kansas City, Missouri, flying *Pete*, at an average speed of 158.16 miles per hour.

In landing after the race, and in a foretaste of what would happen on Sunday, Israel in *Redhead* hit the runway at one hundred miles per hour, and bounced crazily for several hundred yards before he could bring the plane to a stop. Earlier, Roger Don Rae in his Keith Rider Special was not so lucky. After testing his plane and reaching a straightaway speed of 240 miles per hour, Don Rae ran off the south end of the runway and into a drainage ditch, after landing at a speed of more than ninety miles per hour. Don Rae was not hurt, but the landing gear buckled, a wing was damaged, and the propeller bent beyond repair. Don Rae sent to Kansas City for a new propeller, and said he would have the plane repaired in time for the Sunday races.

A late arrival Saturday afternoon in a new Monocoupe was May Haizlip, holder of the speed record for women fliers.

Nine Omaha pilots, some of whom had never raced before, put on a novelty race for the spectators. What they had to do was fly once around the course, land, divest an article of clothing, and then take off again. The pilots divested clothing down to their under shorts (called BVDs in the 1930s), and then reversed the process, putting on an article of clothing after each landing. A.R. "Barney" Burham, flying a Cessna used for the daily weather flights, won the race. His partner, LD. "Dutch" Miller took fourth place.

In the parachute jumping events, Wayne "Mile High" Wagener of Kansas City made an exhibition jump, leaving the plane at twelve thousand feet, and falling over ten thousand feet before pulling the rip cord, trailing flour to mark his fall. In the parachute landing contest, Troy Colboch of Long Beach, California, took first place, landing within three hundred feet of the center of the target. Roger Don Rae was second, landing 393 feet from the target center, followed by Wayne Wagener, third, at 615 feet from the target. During his aerobatics act, Milo Burcham, a Hollywood stunt pilot, lost his engine and had to make a dead-stick landing for an unplanned ending to his routine of rolls, loops, and upside down flying.

Gordon Israel and the Crash of Redhead

The feature event to wind up the 1934 Omaha Air Races was the fifty- mile free-for-all for the Gene Eppley Trophy and a nine hundred dollar first prize ($7,965 in 2002 prices). Israel won the race at an average speed of 197.3 miles per hour, followed by Lee Miles at an average speed of 195.2 miles per hour. For second place he received five hundred dollars ($3,929 in 2002 prices). Art Chester was third, followed by Roger Don Rae in fourth place, and Steve Wittman in fifth place. Last place went to Joe Jacobson, who flew *Pete* at an average speed of 168.8 miles per hour, which was twelve miles an hour faster than his speed in the qualifying races on Saturday.

Israel held a lead until the eighth lap, when with more than a mile lead, he eased up slightly, allowing Lee Miles to pass him at the start of the ninth lap. But Israel pushed his throttle to the wall again, and passed Miles on the far stretch of the same lap. Miles finished about half a mile ahead of Chester, giving him his second win over Chester in a friendly rivalry that they had carried on for eleven races. Afterwards, Chester said, "But I know what my ship needs, and I'll have it done before the National Races."

After winning the feature race, disaster struck the *Redhead* and Israel as he landed after the race, touching down at more than eighty miles an hour. An *Omaha World-Herald* eyewitness reporter described what happened, saying the racer,

> …bounced about 10 feet in the air with its nose up. Then it leveled off, and it seemed that Israel poured on a little bit of gas. The next time the plane hit the ground it was almost level. But apparently the right wheel struck a bump, for the strut or landing gear on that side buckled. The right wing dipped and hit the ground. Then the plane went over on its nose. For a time it stood poised there, its tail straight up in the air. To Israel, as he later admitted, it seemed hours. Then it went over on its back into what seemed an awful mess.

As an ambulance, firemen, and airport workers rushed to the plane, Archie Bailey, in charge of publicity for the races, was first to reach the plane. "Are you hurt?" he asked. "No," Israel replied. "Lift the tail so I can get out."

His younger brother, Ed Israel arrived, and, shouting a warning about fire, helped Bailey lift the tail, while others got Israel out.

Later, Israel said he thought he had made a good three-point landing. "I would have gunned it," he went on, "and taken off again. But it has bounced that way many times before, and I wasn't worried. I would have been all right if I hadn't hit that bump or ditch, or whatever it was."

Lawrence Youngman Comments on the Races

In a long feature article that appeared in the *Omaha World-Herald* on the Monday before the air races began, Lawrence Youngman, aviation reporter for the newspaper, analyzed the subject of air racing in general, while reviewing Omaha's three previous races: 1931, 1932, and 1933.

Looking back on the National Air Races and the Thompson Trophy Race, premier event of those races, Youngman pointed out that in 1929 Doug Davis won the race at an average speed of 194 miles per hour. The next year, Charles "Speed" Holman, who crashed to his death in Omaha in 1931, boosted the average to 204 miles per hour in winning the Thompson Race. Then in 1931, Lowell Bayles, who visited Omaha on a national air tour in 1931, pushed the average up to 236 miles per hour. In 1932 James Doolittle, who never entered the Omaha races, averaged 252.6 miles per hour in winning the Thompson in the stubby, barrel shaped Gee Bee R-1. After winning, Doolittle said he would never fly the tricky Gee Bee again. In 1931 Roscoe Turner came in first with an average speed of 241.0 miles per hour, but was disqualified because he cut a pylon. Thus, Jimmy Wedell, of Wedell-Williams fame, became the winner at an average speed of 237.9 miles per hour. In four years the average speed for the winner in the Thompson Race increased by 22.6 percent, a gain that must be viewed against the fact that these classic racing planes of the 1930s were largely designed and built by the pilots who flew them.

The hazardous life of the racing pilot is reflected in the fact that by 1931, three of these pilots Holman, Bayles, and Wedell were dead. Jimmy Doolittle, well known for leading the raid on Tokyo in March, 1942 during World War II, walked away from air racing after winning the 1932 Thompson Race in the famed Gee Bee.

Imagine, Youngman said, that you:

> ...are at the controls of Benny Howard's little ghost-like racer. The air speed reads two hundred miles per hour—and that's just how fast the pylon is coming your way! ...If you are going to win any prize money, you must get around that pylon at better than 175 miles per hour...if you are doing a decent job of

flying, you'll probably start tilting the plane, lowering the left wing when you are still more than eight hundred feet from the pylon. By the time you are even with the tower, the wings are at a 90-degree angle.

You realize, subconsciously, that this change in position has 'done things' to the flying characteristics of your plane. The controls are 'crossed.' In other words, when the plane is on its side, the rudder becomes the elevator, and the elevator serves as a rudder.

But there's the pylon. You're even with it. Now you ease back on the stick—that's what snaps it around the tower, and maybe, just for luck, you give it a little bottom rudder to keep it from gaining altitude. Like a wild horse sunfishing in midair, it noses around and you are headed the other way. Now all you have to do is straighten up the ol' crate and keep going.

Your thoughts are running something like this: "Well, the wings stayed on for another turn anyway. I thought they would. Gosh, I thought Oscar was going to wham off the tail of my ship with his propeller. Only seven more pylon turns to make. I wish I was a truck driver or something."

Such, in the imagination of Youngman, were the thoughts of an air racing pilot.

Sources and Credits for Photos

About the Author

The 1930 air races in Omaha inspired a love of airplanes and flying for young Wallace Petersen. Petersen served in the Army Air Force for four years during WWII. He earned a private pilot's license and still flies his own Piper Cub J-3.

Petersen retired from his alma-mater, the University of Nebraska-Lincoln, after teaching economics for forty-one years. Biking, building model airplanes and traveling by railroad keep Petersen active and enjoying retirement in Lincoln, Nebraska.

He has a son and a daughter and enjoys spending time with his grandchildren.

Petersen is also the author of seven books on economics.